CRAFT TOPICS

EGYPTIANS

FACTS • THINGS TO MAKE • ACTIVITIES

RACHEL WRIGHT

SEA-TO-SEA
Mankato Collingwood London

This edition first published in 2005 by
Sea-to-Sea Publications
1980 Lookout Drive
North Mankato
Minnesota 56003

ISBN   1-932889-00-0

Printed in China

Library of Congress Control Number: 2004103592

2 4 6 8 9 7 5 3

Published by arrangement with the Watts Publishing Group Ltd, London

Editor: Hazel Poole
Consultant: George Hart, M. Phil
Designed by: Sally Boothroyd
Photography by: Chris Fairclough
Artwork by: Tony Smith
Additional picture research by: Juliet Duff

CONTENTS

THE LAND OF THE PHARAOHS

The first settlers in Egypt lived in small farming communities along the banks of the Nile River. Although the climate was hot and dry, their crops grew easily, thanks to the Nile.

Every year, from July to October, the river flooded its banks. When the water level went down, it left behind a layer of damp, black fertile silt, which was perfect for farming. Before long, the settlers found that they were able to produce plenty of food without too much effort. This gave them more time to weave cloth, make jewelry and carve household goods, all of which helped to improve their standard of living.

THE AGE OF THE PHARAOHS

As time went by, these small communities were joined together, either by agreement or force, until two main kingdoms emerged – one in Lower Egypt, the other in Upper Egypt. In about 3100 BC, these two kingdoms went to war and the victor, King Menes of Upper Egypt, became the first pharaoh of both lands.

By uniting the two kingdoms under a single ruler, Menes paved the way for a more stable and prosperous Egypt. Cities developed, trade flourished, and arts and crafts bloomed. These advances helped to create a rich and cultured way of life, which lasted for about 3,000 years.

► *The Egyptians lived on the fertile land that fringed the Nile. They buried their dead in the desert to the west of the river because this was where the sun set.*

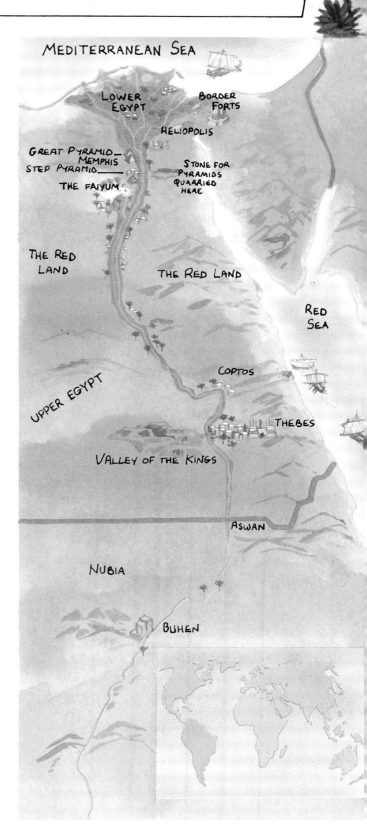

MEDITERRANEAN SEA

LOWER EGYPT

BORDER FORTS

HELIOPOLIS

GREAT PYRAMID
MEMPHIS
STEP PYRAMID
THE FAIYUM

STONE FOR PYRAMIDS QUARRIED HERE

THE RED LAND

THE RED LAND

RED SEA

COPTOS

UPPER EGYPT

THEBES

VALLEY OF THE KINGS

ASWAN

NUBIA

BUHEN

▲ Once a crop had been harvested, cattle trampled on it to separate the grain from the husk. The crop was then tossed into the air so that the lighter husks would blow away, leaving the grain to fall to the ground.

THE RIVER OF LIFE

The Nile was more than just a river to the ancient Egyptians. It was a life-line. It gave them damp fields in which to grow wheat and barley for making bread and beer, and flax for making linen. It created marshes where cattle grazed and water birds lived. It supplied water to drink, fish to eat, and a waterway to travel on.

Even the papyrus reeds that grew near the water's edge were harvested to make paper, furniture, sandals, and small boats. Without the Nile, the ancient Egyptians would not have existed at all.

FROM FEAST TO FAMINE

The Nile kept Egypt alive, but it could also bring death and destruction. If the annual flood rose too high, homes were swept away and people were drowned. If the flood waters were consistently too low, fewer fields could be farmed and a famine might follow.

To protect themselves from such disasters, the Egyptians built dikes and dug reservoirs to store water for later use. They also dug canals to carry water to fields and gardens far away from the river.

MEASURING THE NILE

The Egyptians used nilometers to help them predict the level of each annual flood. A nilometer was simply a scale of notches carved on a stone surface beside the river.

If the water reached the right level for a particular time of year, then all would be well. If the water level was lower than it should have been, the Egyptians restricted the amount of water let out of the reservoirs. If the water level was dangerously high, everyone got ready to retreat to higher ground.

INTO THE WILDERNESS

Although most Egyptians never left the lush, green Nile Valley, some did venture out into the surrounding desert. Hunters went in search of gazelles and lions, miners went to dig for copper, silver, gold, and semiprecious stones, and traders crossed the sands on their way to the Red Sea and the land of Punt.

MAKE A WATER CLOCK

An ancient Egyptian clock was a stone bowl of water with a scale of notches marked inside it and a hole at the bottom. The Egyptians could tell the time by watching the water level as it dropped down past the notches.

You will need: 2 disposable cups of the same size • extra thick sewing needle • pencil • 2 blocks of balsa wood (one about 9 inches long, the other slightly shorter. The shorter block must be at least 2¼ inches wide and the longer block at least ¾ inch wide) • balsa cement • a watch • paint.

1. Make a hole in the middle of the base of one of the cups using the thick sewing needle.

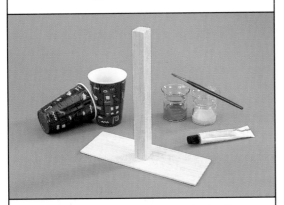

▲ **2.** Decorate both cups with thick undiluted paint and then glue the two blocks of balsa wood together, as shown.

3. Cement the cup with the hole onto the upright block of balsa wood, and place the other cup underneath it.

▲ **4.** When the top cup is stuck firmly in place, cover its hole with your finger and fill it with water. Remove your finger and start timing the water as it drips through the hole.

Using a pencil, mark the level of the water in the top cup at one minute intervals.

5. If you want to double check that your clock is accurate, empty the water from the bottom cup into the top one. Wait until the water level reaches the first notch and start timing again.

THE PHARAOH'S PEOPLE

The pharaoh was the most important person in ancient Egypt. Although he was human, his people believed that he was also a god, complete with godlike powers.

The pharaoh owned everything in the land, including the people. He was the head of the government, the army, and the law courts, as well as being a link between his people and the gods. Yet, although his word was law, he did not rule alone. Wealthy nobles were given top government jobs, and a vast number of officials were appointed to collect taxes, organize defense, and check that everything ran smoothly.

As the Egyptians did not use money, taxes were paid in the form of crops, goods, and physical labor. These taxes were then used for the upkeep of the state and for paying everyone's wages.

◄ The white crown of Upper Egypt was worn with the red crown of Lower Egypt to show that the pharaoh was ruler of both kingdoms.

A PYRAMID OF PEOPLE

Ancient Egyptian society was structured like a pyramid. At the top was the pharaoh. Next in line were the nobles, priests, army officers, and government officials. Below them came the merchants, artists, and specialist craftsmen. Most of these craftsmen worked together in large organized workshops or special villages, and were employed by the pharaoh, his nobles, or the temples.

► This gold death mask was made for Tutankhamen by Egyptian craftsmen. Tutankhamen was only nine when he became pharaoh, and he ruled for less than ten years.

▲ A craftsmen's workshop. In the top left of the picture, a worker weighs gold before issuing it to the craftsmen. The two men below him present some finished work for inspection. The men on the top row are carpenters. Those below are jewelers and goldsmiths.

▶ Slaves serving at a banquet.

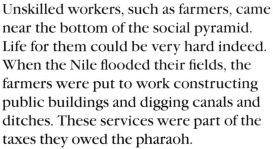

Unskilled workers, such as farmers, came near the bottom of the social pyramid. Life for them could be very hard indeed. When the Nile flooded their fields, the farmers were put to work constructing public buildings and digging canals and ditches. These services were part of the taxes they owed the pharaoh.

Although farmers were often very poor, they had the right to rent land and keep animals. Egypt's slaves were also allowed to have land and possessions, but, unlike the farmers, they were not legally free. Many slaves were prisoners of war. Some of them worked as servants in the houses of the rich. Others were sent out into the desert to mine for gold.

EGYPT'S CHILDREN

Most Egyptians could neither read nor write. Boys from the lower classes were probably taught a trade or craft by their fathers, while the girls were taught how to run a household by their mothers. On the whole, it was mainly the sons of privileged men who learned to read and write and do arithmetic.

SCHOLARS AND SCRIBES

Reading, writing, and arithmetic were very important to the Egyptians. The government, army, and temples all needed professional writers and mathematicians who could organize others and keep a record of day-to-day business. The men they employed to do this work were called scribes.

Scribal training was a long and difficult task. Would-be scribes spent most of their childhood in a schoolroom, copying and chanting texts. They practiced writing on pieces of stone and broken pot using reed brushes or pens dipped in ink. Only later, when they were fully qualified, were they given expensive papyrus to write on instead.

Although scribal education must have been very boring at times, it paid off in the end. Scribes were always in great demand and many of them rose to positions of power in the government and priesthood. One scribe even managed to become a god!

▲ Most scribes kept their reed brushes in a wooden palette like this. The holes at the top were used for ink.

WRITING

Scribes wrote using picture symbols called hieroglyphs. There were about 700 hieroglyphs in all.

Some hieroglyphs represented whole words such as the picture shown here meaning "life." Others represented only one or two letters.

ANKH

Hieroglyphic writing was extremely elaborate. It had no vowels, no punctuation, and could be read from top to bottom, from left to right, or from right to left. No wonder it took scholars so long to master it!

▼ Hieroglyphs were used on tombs and monuments, but business documents and letters were written in a simpler, quicker script called hieratic.

B FOOT

CH TETHERING ROPE

D HAND

F HORNED VIPER

G JAR STAND

H PLAN VIEW OF HUT

H TWISTED FLAX

I FLOWERING REED

J SNAKE

K BASKET

M OWL

N WATER

P MAT

Q HILL SLOPE

R MOUTH

S FOLDED CLOTH

SH POOL

T LOAF

W QUAIL CHICK

Z DOOR BOLT

MAKE A SCARAB STAMP SEAL

▶ *The Egyptians used seals to stamp information on clay or papyrus. Scarabs, representing the god of the sun, were often carved on the top of these seals.*

You will need: modeling clay • a ballpoint pen • rolling pin • craft knife • ink pad • cookie sheet.

Ask a grown-up to help you.

TO MAKE THE TOP OF THE SEAL

▲ **1.** Model a beetle out of clay, keeping its base as flat as possible.

TO MAKE THE UNDERSIDE OF THE SEAL

▲ **2.** Roll out some modeling clay, the same shape as your beetle, and carve a message on it using the tip of a ballpoint pen. You can either invent some picture writing or use hieroglyphs shown on this page. Make sure that you carve each word backward, otherwise your message will print backward!

3. When you've finished carving, check that the slab of clay is perfectly flat, and then join both parts of your seal together.

4. Put your seal on a cookie sheet and bake it in the oven at 300°F for 10 minutes.

5. When your seal has cooled, press it down on the ink pad and then press it on some paper.

GODS AND GODDESSES

The ancient Egyptians worshipped hundreds of different gods. They had domestic gods whose statues were placed in the home to bring good luck to the family, local gods who were called upon to take care of a particular town, and national gods, such as the sun god, Re, who were glorified throughout Egypt.

Although each of the major gods had a huge temple built in his or her honor, ordinary worshippers were not allowed far beyond the entrance. Instead, they had to dictate their prayers and requests to a priest, who passed their messages on to the god for them.

▲ *Pharaoh Ramses II (1304 – 1237 BC) had this rock-cut temple built at Abu Simbel in Nubia.*

▼ *A bronze model of the crocodile god, Sebek. Sacred crocodiles living in the temple at Crocodilopolis were covered with jewels and pampered by priests. When they died, their scaly bodies were mummified.*

ANIMAL WORSHIP

Most gods were associated with animals because the Egyptians revered and feared many of the birds and beasts that shared their world. For them, the falcon with its power of flight was something to marvel at, and an ideal symbol for their sky god, Horus. The wild bull with its immense strength represented Ptah, the creator of the world. And the crocodile lurking in the Nile symbolized the water god, Sebek. Man-eating crocodiles were a constant threat to the Egyptians, which may explain why they were worshipped. After all, if you turn your enemy into a god, your enemy may be less tempted to turn you into a snack!

Not all gods took on the shape of an animal. As the Egyptians became more sophisticated, they began to feel less in awe of the animals around them. As a result, they started worshipping gods in human or part human form, as well. For example, Isis, the goddess of women, was often shown as a woman wearing cow horns.

MAGIC AND MYSTERY

Religion and superstition were closely linked, and many Egyptians wore magic charms, or amulets, to ward off evil. Even children sometimes put fish-shaped charms in their hair, to guard against drowning.

MAKE A FISH CHARM

You will need: cardboard • air-hardening modeling material • glue • bobby pins • acrylic paint • clear nail polish • pencil • scissors.

1. Draw the outline of a fish on a piece of cardboard and cut the shape out.

▲ **2.** Using modeling material, make a teardrop-shaped body for your fish. Try to keep the underside of this shape as flat as possible.

3. Wait for the modeling material to dry, and then glue both parts of your fish together and paint it.

▲ **4.** When the paint has dried, glue or tape a bobby pin onto the back of your fish and coat the whole thing, except the bobby pin, with clear nail polish.

EGYPTIAN MUMMIES

The Egyptians believed in life after death. They also believed that the dead would need their bodies in this afterlife, and so they invented mummification to preserve corpses from decay.

Mummification was a very expensive process. Some people could only afford certain stages of the treatment. Others could not afford it at all and were simply buried in the sand when they died. Only the very rich were mummified properly.

UNDER WRAPS

When a wealthy person died, their body was taken to an embalmer's workshop. There the brain was pulled out through the nose with a bronze hook and thrown away. The stomach, lungs, intestines, and liver were also taken out of the body but, unlike the brain, they were dried out, wrapped in linen and put in containers called canopic jars. The heart, thought to be the center of intelligence, was left in the body.

After the inner organs had been removed, the body was covered with a salt called natron, to dry it out and keep it from rotting. It was then washed, packed with natron and linen, covered with oils, and wrapped in linen bandages. Magical spells were often written on the bandages to safeguard the dead person on their way to the afterlife.

When the mummy was finally wrapped and ready, it was put into a coffin and taken to the tomb. Priests performed rituals to ensure that the dead person would be able to walk and talk in the next life. This whole process – from the start of the embalming to the end of the religious ceremonies – took about 70 days.

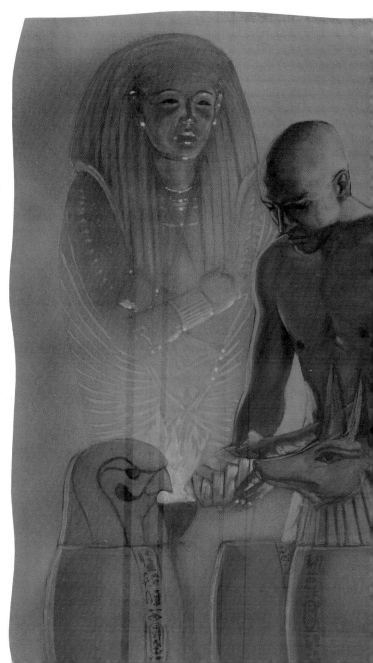

▶ *Preparing the dead for burial can't have been much fun. Apart from the terrible smell of rotting flesh, the embalmers had to put up with rats scuttling around their feet and flies buzzing around the corpse.*

14

JOURNEY TO ANOTHER WORLD

Bandaging bodies was a smelly business, but it was nowhere near as hazardous as the journey the dead made on their way to the afterlife. They had to cross the River of Death, face fiends, and stand trial for their sins. Before Osiris, the god of the dead, and a jury of 42, the deceased's heart was weighed against the Feather of Truth and Rightfulness. If the scales balanced, the deceased was welcomed into the next life. If the scales tilted, he was devoured by a monstrous creature and destroyed forever.

► *The jackal-headed god, Anubis, weighs the heart of a dead person against the Feather of Truth and Rightfulness.*

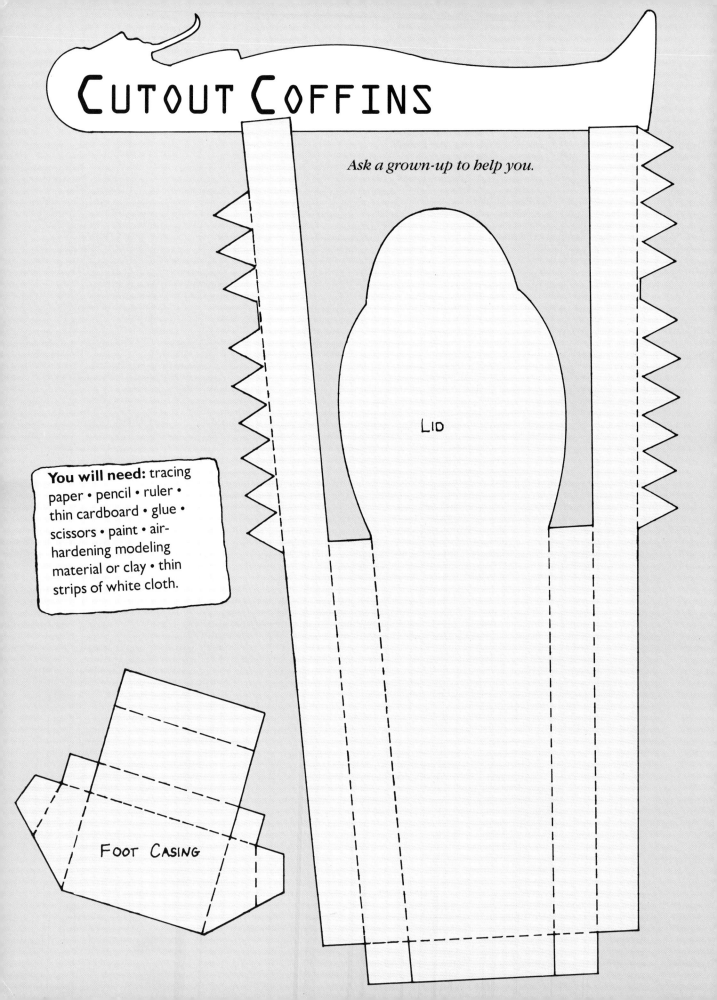

CUTOUT COFFINS

Ask a grown-up to help you.

LID

You will need: tracing paper • pencil • ruler • thin cardboard • glue • scissors • paint • air-hardening modeling material or clay • thin strips of white cloth.

FOOT CASING

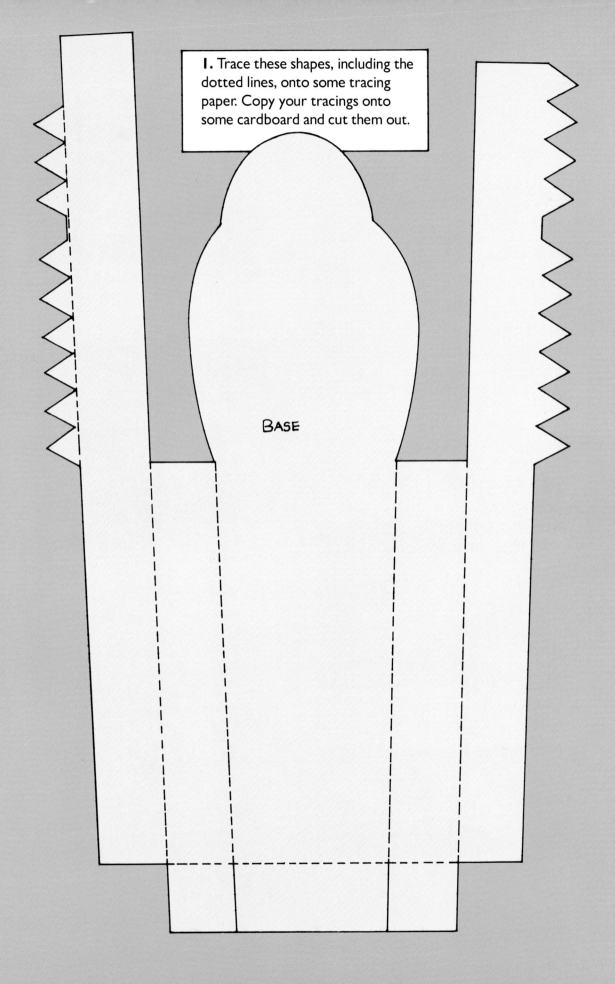

I. Trace these shapes, including the dotted lines, onto some tracing paper. Copy your tracings onto some cardboard and cut them out.

BASE

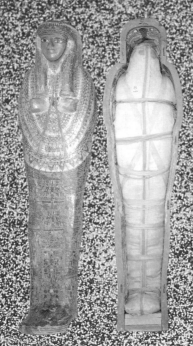

TO MAKE THE LID

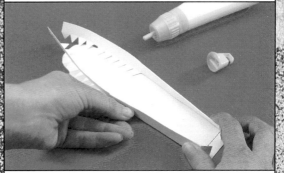

▲ **5.** Glue both sides of the lid down in the same way as you glued the sides of the base.

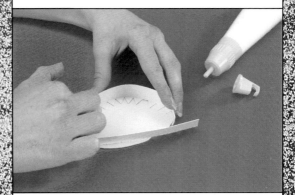

▲ **6.** Glue the bottom end of the lid together and then stick all the remaining tabs to the inside of the lid as shown.

2. Using a ruler to guide you, gently run the tip of your scissors along all the dotted lines on your cardboard shapes. This will make the cardboard easier to fold.

TO MAKE THE BASE OF THE COFFIN

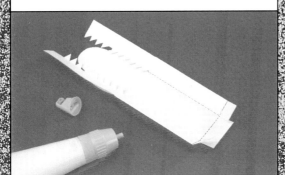

▲ **3.** Glue the two outer panels down as shown, and fold them inward.

▲ **4.** Glue the bottom end of the coffin together, and then glue all the remaining tabs to the inside of the base.

TO MAKE A CASING FOR THE MUMMY'S FEET

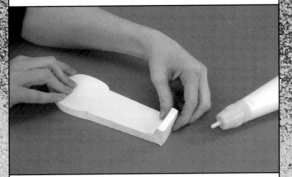

▲ **7.** Fold along all the dotted lines. Glue the four tabs to the inside of the casing, and then glue the whole casing to the bottom end of the lid.

8. If you can, have a look at photographs of real mummy coffins before you paint your model. You may see some signs and symbols that would look good on your coffin.

TO MAKE A MUMMY

9. Mold a figure out of modeling material and leave it somewhere warm to dry. When it has hardened, cover it with glue and wind thin strips of cloth around it. Make sure the cloth dries out properly before you lay your mummy to rest in its coffin.

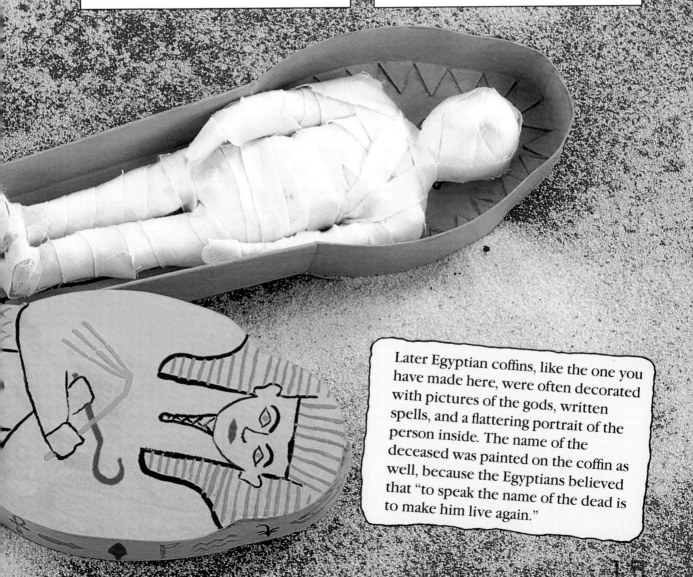

Later Egyptian coffins, like the one you have made here, were often decorated with pictures of the gods, written spells, and a flattering portrait of the person inside. The name of the deceased was painted on the coffin as well, because the Egyptians believed that "to speak the name of the dead is to make him live again."

HOMES FOR THE DEAD

The Egyptians believed that life after death was like life on earth, only a lot more peaceful! So, they crammed their tombs with everything they might need to enjoy the afterlife in comfort. Some of these objects came from their homes, others were made especially for the tomb. Nobles were often buried with small statues of servants, in the hope that these models would spring to life in the next world and keep their owners fed and cared for.

Unlike the rich, the poor did not travel into the next life armed with treasures. Most of them were buried with only scraps of food and a small selection of useful possessions.

EVERLASTING HOMES

The tombs of the rich and famous were like palaces. Some had chapels and courtyards, and chambers that were decorated with colorful paintings. Many of these paintings showed activities that their dead owner had enjoyed in this life and hoped, by means of magic, to continue doing in the next.

A wealthy Egyptian took as much care decorating his tomb as he did his home. This is because he regarded the tomb as an everlasting home, to which his spirit would return from time to time.

▼ *The interior of a wealthy Egyptian's tomb.*

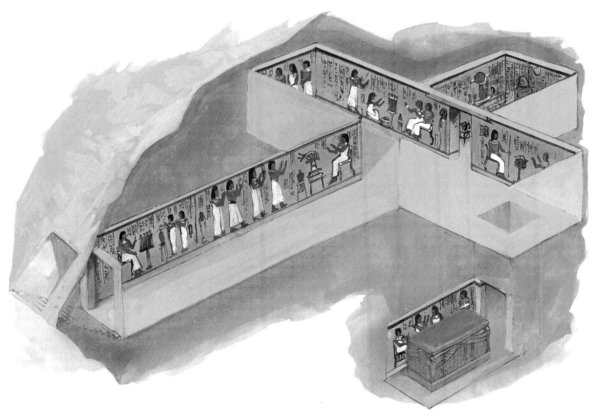

ROYAL TOMBS

The most magnificent tombs of all belonged to the pharaohs. Some of the early pharaohs were buried deep inside stone pyramids. These mighty monuments could take up to 20 years to build. Gangs of unskilled workers had to drag each block of stone up mud ramps to the level where it was needed, and then lever it into position.

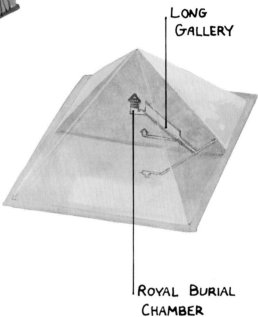

LONG GALLERY

ROYAL BURIAL CHAMBER

ROBBERS OF THE DEAD

Magical texts promised death and disaster to anyone who tried to plunder the pyramids. Yet despite these curses, tomb robbing became common, and pharaohs were forced to abandon pyramids in favor of better protected graves.

The new royal tombs were cut deep into the sides of a remote desert valley on the west bank of the Nile. But even though these rock-cut tombs were less conspicuous than the pyramids, thieves soon broke their way in and emptied them of their treasures. Only the royal tomb of Tutankhamen escaped the thieves. It was discovered in 1922 by an archaeologist named Howard Carter.

► *The pyramids of Giza. The largest of these pyramids is known as the Great Pyramid. 450 feet high, it was built in about 2528 BC for King Khufu. The smaller pyramids in front of it were built for Khufu's three main wives.*

HOMES FOR THE LIVING

To avoid the summer floods, Egyptian towns and villages were usually built on high ground. However, as towns grew up, land for building became scarce, and tall, narrow townhouses had to be built very close together. The families who lived in these houses often cooked and slept on the roof to get away from the heat and dust of the crowded streets below.

OUT IN THE COUNTRY

To escape the hustle and bustle of town life, wealthy Egyptians built themselves roomy, elegant villas on the outskirts of town. In each of these villas, the women's quarters, bedrooms, and bathroom were arranged around a central room, which was used for entertaining guests. The servant's quarters, kitchens, stables, and granaries all stood outside the villa, protected by a wall.

Shade was a real luxury for the Egyptians and cool, columned porches and tree-shaded gardens were an essential part of any rich man's home. Many villa gardens also had a decorative pool, full of fish and lotus lilies.

▼ The gardens of the rich were more than just decorative. They provided fruit, such as figs and dates, as well as vegetables. Pottery beehives were often kept in the grounds of a villa, too. The Egyptians used honey to sweeten their food. The conical containers in the foreground are granaries, used for storing grain.

BUILDING BRICKS

Nearly all Egyptian houses, even the pharaoh's palace, were made of mud bricks. The sticky Nile mud was mixed with straw or sand, shaped into bricks, and left out in the sun to dry.

▶ *This model shows the type of house a country farmer might have lived in. Food would have been stored in the courtyard, and the cooking may well have been done on the roof to reduce the risk of fire. As in all Egyptian houses, the small window was set high up to keep the rooms inside as cool as possible.*

FURNITURE

Egyptian homes were less cluttered with furniture than ours. In fact, poor people had virtually no furniture at all, and used reed mats and mattresses instead of chairs and beds. The rich often sat on the floor, too, but they had folding stools or, if they were lucky, low chairs to sit on as well. Neither the rich nor the poor had wardrobes or closets. Everyone stored their belongings in chests.

Like most furniture, the beds of the wealthy were made from wood and reeds. Even the pillows were made from wood! These wooden headrests were, in fact, a lot more comfortable than they might seem. By raising a sleeper's head off the bed, they helped to keep the neck both cool and clear of snakes and scorpions.

▼ *This furniture once belonged to Queen Hetepheres I. The headrest would have had a cushion on it, and the bed had linen covers.*

CLOTHES AND COSMETICS

Nearly all Egyptian clothes were made from linen, which varied in quality. Most people wore coarse linen, but the rich wore fabric so soft and fine it was almost see-through.

DRESS STYLES

In general, women wore a long, straight dress with shoulder straps, and men wore a piece of linen tied at the waist. Children often wore nothing at all, particularly during the summer months. For hot and heavy outdoor work, men usually wore a loincloth, and women wore a short skirt.

HAIR CARE

Rich and fashionable Egyptians wore elaborate wigs made from real hair and vegetable fibers. Everyone else simply left their shaved heads bare or wore their hair very short. Children often had shaved heads too, except for a ponytail on the right side of their head called "the lock of youth."

SKIN CARE

Both men and women used oils and creams to keep their skin from becoming dry in the hot desert sun. They also used makeup to protect their eyes and lips from the sun, sand, and dust. Eyeshadows and lip paints were made from minerals which were ground into a powder, mixed with oil or water, and then applied with fingers or fine sticks.

CLOTH COLLARS

▶ *The Egyptians loved to wear plenty of brightly colored jewelry. Neck collars, like the one shown here, were worn by both men and women. The rows of beads were made from clay, gold, glass, and semiprecious stones.*

You will need: a circle of thick cloth measuring 16 inches across (felt is a good fabric to use because it doesn't fray) • pencil/pen • scissors • ruler • glue • velcro • beads • braiding • nutshells, etc., for decoration.

▲ **1.** Draw a circle measuring 5 inches across in the middle of your cloth. Cut out the smaller circle and put it to one side.

▲ **2.** Now cut away slightly less than a quarter of your cloth collar as shown. If the cloth starts to fray, turn the edges onto the other side of the collar and glue them down.

▲ **3.** Glue a strip of velcro to each end of the collar. One strip needs to go on the upper side of the collar, the other on the underside.

4. Stick buttons, beads, painted nutshells, ribbons, or anything else you can think of onto your collar to decorate it.

MAKE AN EGYPTIAN WIG

You will need: Two 2-ounce balls of chunky black yarn • a circle of dark colored cloth (preferably felt) measuring 12 inches across • a strip of felt long enough to go around your head with a bit to spare • a piece of thick cardboard the same size as this page • chalk • tape • tape measure • white glue • needle threaded with black yarn.

Ask a friend to help you.

If you have long hair, pin it in a flat bun at the back of your neck so that it doesn't stick out from under your wig.

▲ **3.** Now cut through the yarn at one end of the cardboard, and glue the folded end of each strand to your strip of felt. Make sure you leave a gap for your face in the center of the headband, as well as a small gap at either end.

4. When your headband is complete, check that it fits, and glue it together.

▲ **1.** Tape one end of a ball of yarn to your piece of cardboard and then wind the yarn around the cardboard as shown.

2. When you've covered the cardboard with yarn, cut the final strand and tape it to the cardboard.

▲ **5.** Put the circle of dark cloth on top of your head, and ask a friend to slide the headband into position over it.

▲ **6.** Your friend now needs to draw the position of the top edge of the headband onto the circle of cloth. They should use some chalk to do this.

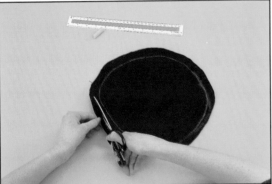

▲ **7.** When your friend has finished, take the wig off your head. Cut out the oval shape they have drawn, leaving about ¾ inch of extra material all the way around.

▲ **8.** Smear some glue around the inside edge of your chalk oval and then glue strands of yarn across it. Keep doing this until the fabric is completely covered.

9. To make a part, sew a line of yarn stitches down the center of the oval.

10. Put the cloth oval on your head again and ask your friend to dab some glue along the side of the headband and slide it into position. They may need to fold the oval slightly in places, to make it fit.

11. If the ends of the wig are uneven, ask your friend to trim them.

THE END OF ANCIENT EGYPT

The deserts and seas surrounding ancient Egypt acted like barriers, and for over a thousand years they protected the country from foreign invasion. This enabled the Egyptians to develop their unique way of life without interference from other cultures.

However, despite this natural protection, Egypt was eventually attacked, and from the 900s BC onward, it was ruled by a series of powerful invaders.

In 332 BC the Egyptians were conquered by the Greek ruler, Alexander the Great. He opened up Egypt to a wider world by building a fabulous trading city on the Mediterranean coast. This city, called Alexandria, soon became so famous that people flocked there from far and wide to exchange ideas and goods.

▲ The Greeks ruled Egypt for 300 years. The last of the Egyptian queens was Queen Cleopatra. When her army was defeated by the Romans in 30 BC, she killed herself.

In 30 BC Egypt was taken over by the Romans, and became part of their empire. When the Roman Empire later converted to Christianity, Egypt converted too. The coming of Christianity marked the end of the ancient Egyptian world. Temples were replaced by churches and monasteries, and many of the old ways and beliefs were abandoned forever.

When the Arabs invaded in the 600s AD, Egypt became a mainly Muslim country, as it is today.

DID YOU KNOW?

At one time it was fashionable in Egypt for party-goers to wear a cone of perfumed grease on their heads. As it became hotter, the grease melted and drenched their clothes in sweet smelling oil.

Egyptian mummies have been put to some very strange uses over the years. In medieval times, they were powdered down and used as medicine. In the 1800s, a shipload of cat mummies was sent to England and turned into fertilizer. The American writer Mark Twain, claimed that mummies were even used to stoke Egyptian railroad engines!

To make papyrus, the Egyptians first peeled away the outer skin of the papyrus reed.

Next they cut the inner stem into strips . . .

. . . and arranged a horizontal layer of strips over a vertical layer.

Then they covered the strips with linen, and pounded them with a mallet to make them stick together.

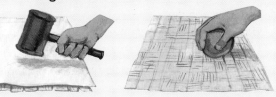

Finally they polished the sheet with a stone and rolled it up into a scroll.

The ancient Egyptians were the first people to divide the year into 365 days and 12 months. They were also the first people to divide each day into 24 hours.

Glossary

Archaeologist – someone who studies life in ancient times.

BC – Before Christ. 3100 BC means 3,100 years before the birth of Christ. The letters AD stand for "Anno Domini," which is latin for "in the year of our Lord." 1992 AD means 1,992 years after the birth of Christ.

Canopic jars – containers into which the stomach, lungs, intestines, and liver were placed during mummification. Each of the four canopic jars had the head of a god carved on its lid, to protect the organ inside.

Dike – a mound built to prevent flooding.

Embalmer – someone who treats a dead body with chemicals to keep it from decaying.

Flax – a stringy plant used for making linen. The stems of the plant were washed, separated, and twisted together to make thread. The thread was then woven on a loom to make linen.

Gazelle – Small antelope.

Land of Punt – no one is sure where this land was, but it seems probable that it was somewhere near the Red Sea, perhaps in Somalia. The Egyptians obtained incense from the people of Punt.

Natron – a salt found in the Egyptian desert.

Papyrus – tall water reed. The word "papyrus" also refers to the actual writing material the Egyptians made from papyrus reeds.

Pharaoh – ruler of ancient Egypt. The title "pharaoh" means "the Great House."

Revere – to respect or hold in great awe.

Scarab – a sacred beetle.

Silt – fine mud made up of minerals, dead plants, and other organic pieces that water gathers as it flows.

RESOURCES

BOOKS TO READ

Egyptian Gods and Goddesses by Henry Barker (New York; Grosset & Dunlap, 1999)

Ancient Egyptians and their Neighbors by Maria Broida (Chigago; Chicago Museum Press, 1999)

Off the Wall Museum Guides for Kids: Egyptian Art by Janice Lehmberg (New York, Sterling, 1998)

Mummies and Pyramids by Will and Ma Osborne (New York; Random House Books for Young Readers, 2001)

Write Like an Ancient Egyptian by Scholastic Inc. Staff (New York, Scholastic, 2003)

The Egyptian News by Scott Steedman (Boston; Candlewich Books, 2000)

You Wouldn't Want to be an Egyptian Mummy! By David Stewart (New York; Franklin Watts, 2000)

PLACES TO VISIT

The Brooklyn Museum
Eastern Parkway
Brooklyn, NY 11238
(718) 638-5000
The Egyptian collection consists of numerous artifacts, including carved statuettes, paintings, a quartzite statue of Pharaoh Akhenaten's daughter, Princess Maket-aten, and much more.

The Cleveland Museum of Art
11150 East Boulevard at University
    Circle
Cleveland, Ohio 44160
(216) 421-7340
This museum displays such items as carved wall reliefs, a limestone pharaoh portrait, statuettes, bronze and silver, and one of the oldest excavated works – an alabaster sculpture of the frog goddess, Hequat.

Metropolitan Museum of Art
Fifth Avenue at 82nd Street
New York, NY 10028
(212) 535-7710
Among the many and varied items to be viewed are gold objects, jewelry and headdresses, mummy cases, sculpture, an ancient temple and tomb, and other excavated pieces such as a statue of Pharaoh Hatshepsut, stone statuettes, vessels, and much much more.

Boston Museum of Fine Arts
465 Huntington Avenue
Boston, Massachusetts 02115
(617) 267-9300
Egyptian antiquities such as sculptured busts can be seen on display, as well as a standing figure of Pharaoh Mycerinus, builder of the third of the great pyramids at Giza.

Rosicrucian Egyptian Museum
Rosicrucian Park
San Jose, California 95191
This museum is actually a replica of an Egyptian temple, and contains a very large collection of artifacts including clay figures and carved animals.

INDEX

Additional photographs: Ancient Art & Architecture Collection 10(t), 12(t); reproduced by courtesy of the Trustees of the British Museum 13(t); Michael Holford 7(t), 9(t), 12(b), 15(tr), 18(tl), 29(r); Peter Clayton 10(b), 11(t), 23(t); Werner Forman Archive 23(b), 25, 29(tl); Zefa 8(br), 21(br).